GW00319292

LITTLE BOOK OF
HORSES

Written by Jon Stroud

LITTLE BOOK OF
HORSES

First published in the UK in 2010

© G2 Entertainment Limited 2014

www.G2ent.co.uk

Printed and bound in Europe

ISBN 978-1-782812-57-9

Contents

Introduction

When we look back through the pages of history it is hard to imagine how man could possibly have survived had it not been for his unique and longstanding relationship with the horse. In his service the horse has fearlessly carried knights into battle. It has pulled the plough and the cart for the humble farmer. It has been the mount of kings and generals. It has carried the mail across the plains of America, towed canal barges filled with coal to Britain's industrial heartland and driven fresh fish from the Channel ports to the Paris dinner table.

Today we have the internal combustion engine, jet air travel and the internet but 100 years ago the global economy was driven by one thing – horse power. Without the horse the world would be a very different place from the one we live in today.

Its contribution to man's success has not gone without recognition. Beautiful in appearance and elegant in motion, since ancient times the noble horse has been the subject of poetry, prose, paintings and sculpture.

Today there are 1.4 million horses in the United Kingdom and more than four times that in the United States but, whilst the horse can still be found hard at work in some parts of the world, most enjoy an existence providing pleasure and sport for their dedicated and loving owners – a just reward for all those years of hard service at man's beck and call.

Jumping

History

The first true jumping competition was organised by the Royal Dublin Society as part of the Dublin Show in 1869.

Held on the lawns of the magnificent Leinster House, the "leaping contest", as it was then known, incorporated three competitions – a high leap over gorse trimmed hurdles, a wide leap over a 30in gorse-filled hurdle in front of 12ft of water and a wall jump over a loose stone wall not exceeding 6ft with a first prize of £5 for each class and a trophy for the overall winner. Judging at this time was, however, somewhat arbitrary with the only proviso being that obstacles had to be cleared "to the satisfaction of the judges". In 1881 the first continuous course was introduced. Such was its popularity there were a phenomenal 800 entries forcing organisers to set off competitors two at a time!

This new and exciting sport proved to be popular with riders and spectators alike and was quick to take off. It appeared in the Olympics for the first time at the 1900 Paris Games where Belgian, Aimé Haageman, finished first of 37 competitors from five nations who contested the 22 jumps over an 850m timed course. Also, for the one and only time in Olympic history there was an equestrian long jump and an equestrian high jump.

The burgeoning sport was given a further boost when a show jumping class was included in the programme of the inaugural International Horse Show at London Olympia in 1907. The majority of the participants were of an army background; however, it stimulated sufficient interest in the sport to open the way for other riders of a non-military background to take part.

The Modern Competition

Each national equestrian federation has its own specific rules governing jumping classes. In high level competitions riders will jump a course of 12 jumps of varying height, width and construction from a simple upright to combination jumps and sometimes even water obstacles or banks. Riders are required to complete the course taking the jumps in a specific order whilst staying within a prescribed time limit.

Should a combination of horse and rider knock down a jump, suffer a refusal, fall or exceed the time limit,

JUMPING

Penalties Awarded In Show Jumping	
First disobedience	4 penalties
Obstacle knocked down while jumping	4 penalties
One or more feet in water jump or any imprint on the lath defining the limit on the landing side	4 penalties
First fall of a competitor or horse or both	Elimination
Second disobedience or other infringement	Elimination
Exceeding the time allowed in the first and second rounds and jump-offs not against the clock	1 penalty point for every four seconds commenced
Exceeding the time allowed in a jump-off against the clock	1 penalty for each second or commenced fraction of a second

penalty points are awarded. A clear round is awarded when horse and rider finish with zero penalties within the time.

As it is not uncommon for more than one rider to complete the first round "clear" the competition usually progresses to a second round called a "jump-off". All qualifying riders are then required to jump again for which the same course is used, albeit with several of the jumps removed. This second round is run against the clock. The overall winner is the combination of horse and rider that finish with the lowest accumulated penalty points in the shortest time possible.

Other types of jumping events include "speed horse" competitions which are run in a single round against the clock, "accumulators" where penalties are not awarded but points are depending on the difficulty of the jump (the rider with the highest score being the winner) and the Puissance. Sometimes known as "the big red wall", riders jump successive rounds over an obstacle of increasing height – the winner being the rider whose horse jumps the highest. The world record in the Puissance is 2.39m.

Dressage

History

Dressage is the ultimate expression of horse and rider working together in perfect harmony and is seen as the basic groundwork for all other disciplines. Its origins lie with the teachings of the Greek general Xenophon (430-354 BC) whose work, *On Horsemanship*, was the inspiration behind the formation of the Naples riding academy in 1532 and the writing of *Le Manège Royal* a century later. This taught how a rider could learn to understand the character of his horse and, in doing so, win over its willing cooperation.

There followed the development of Classical Dressage which, whilst undeniably an art form, was based upon movements required on the battlefield. This evolved into the *Haute École* form of dressage including its world famous "airs above the ground" in which horse and rider perform the physically demanding *levade, courbette* and *capriole*, the latter requiring the horse to leap high into the air whilst kicking out with his hind legs. Whilst this High School of dressage is now largely consigned to the past it is still demonstrated by a select few riding schools including the famous Spanish Riding School of Vienna, the Royal Andalusian School of Equestrian Art in Jerez, Spain and the Cadre Noir in Saumur, France.

Although the art of dressage was avidly practised and followed by countless proponents, it was not until 1873 that the first dressage competition was held in Vienna and a further 29 years

The Modern Competition

Thankfully there are no barrels involved in modern day dressage. Performing in a level arena measuring 40m x 20m or 60m x 20m, riders are required to complete a series of predetermined movements, known as figures, to the satisfaction of a judge or panel of judges who are stationed at set positions outside the arena. The arena itself is skirted by low boards and a set of lettered markers which serve to identify where each figure should start and finish.

Each movement is scored out of 10 with additional points, known as the collective marks, being awarded for the freedom and regularity of the paces, the horse's impulsion (its ability to move forward and engagement of the hindquarters), its submission and the rider's own position and seat. The overall mark is then converted into a percentage to give the final score. Should two riders finish on an identical score then the rider with the highest collective mark is declared the winner.

until the first international competition took place in Turin, Italy. With equestrian sports gaining in popularity it was included as part of the 1912 Stockholm Olympics where cavalry officer Count Carl Gustaf Bonde, representing the home nation, took the gold medal riding Emperor. The format of the competition, however, bore little similarity to what we see today and included jumping several small obstacles including a barrel which was rolled in the direction of the horse!

Dressage has remained on the Oympic programme ever since and has grown into a high profile sport practised worldwide.

Gaining in popularity is the freestyle, otherwise known as the kür, in which horse and rider perform a choreographed routine set to a musical accompaniment. Although there is a requirement to include a series of compulsory movements it does allow riders to create a routine that can play to the best abilities of their horse.

Fei Dressage Test Levels *(all performed in a 60m x 20m arena)*	
Prix St Georges	Medium standard
Intermediare 1	Relatively advanced standard
Intermediare 2	Advanced standard
Grand Prix	A demanding five and a half minute test requiring all of the basic movements plus the fundamental airs of the Classical High School including pirouettes, piaffe, passage and flying lead changes
Grand Prix Special	A seven minute test requiring the same movements as Grand Prix with increased focus on the advanced movements
Grand Prix Freestyle (Kür)	A freestyle routine to music utilising all of the Grand Prix movements

Eventing

History

Also know as horse trials, the sport of eventing traces its roots back to military origins where cavalry competitions were used to test the speed, endurance, scope and obedience of horses and the overall technical ability of their riders. At this time the discipline was known simply as the "Military".

The first true competition was held in 1902. Designed to be a test of dressage, jumping and endurance and open only to serving army officers, the *Championnat du Cheval d'Armes* was the brainchild of the French *inspecteur de cavalerie* General Donop. It included dressage at the Bois de Boulogne, a 50km endurance ride at the Forêt de Marly to the west of Paris, a steeplechase on the racecourse at Auteuil and a jumping competition at the Grand Palais in the heart of the capital. Vichy and Fontainebleau were quick to follow with competitions of their own and steadily the exciting format began to gain interest.

When the Military was first included at the Olympic Games in 1912, entries were still restricted to serving members of the armed forces. Held over five consecutive days, riders were required to complete a 55km endurance ride within 4 hours, negotiate 12 obstacles over a 5km cross-country course in 15 minutes, cover a 3,500m steeplechase course with 10 obstacles in 5 minutes 50 seconds, jump 15 obstacles up to 1.30m high and 3.00m wide before finally completing a dressage test.

It was only after the Second World War that male civilians and then finally women were permitted to compete in the sport of eventing – its biggest boost coming from the creation by the 10th Duke of Beaufort of the Badminton Horse Trials. Held annually since 1949 at the stunning Beaufort estate in Gloucestershire, it remains to this day the highest profile and most prestigious eventing competition on the international calendar.

The Modern Competition

Contested over either one or three days depending on the level of competition, modern eventing consists of a dressage phase, a cross-country phase and a jumping phase.

As with any dressage competition, the object of the first phase is to assess the horse's obedience, flexibility and paces and its harmony with the rider by means of a series of compulsory movements; with many eventing horses already keen to progress to the galloping pace and wide open spaces

of the cross-country this is often not as straightforward as it may seem! Riders are awarded a penalty mark based upon their performance.

For many years the cross-country phase included not only the timed cross-country but also steeplechase and road and track (endurance) stages. Whilst a small number of three-day events are

Basic Penalties Awarded In Cross-Country	
First refusal, circle or run-out at an obstacle	20 penalties
Second refusal, circle or run-out at same obstacle	40 penalties
Third refusal, circle or run-out anywhere on course	Elimination
Fall of horse or rider	Elimination
Exceeding optimum time	0.4 penalties per second
Finishing under speed fault time	0.4 penalties per second
Exceeding time limit (2x optimum time)	Elimination

and World Championship, have moved to what is commonly termed the "short format" competition.

The cross-country course itself incorporates anything from a dozen jumping efforts at the lowest levels of competition to 30 or even 40 at the very highest levels. Obstacles are of a solid construction and can include stone walls, gates, woodpiles, ditches and water. The object is to complete the course within a prescribed optimum time without incurring penalty points which may be awarded for run-outs, refusals or exceeding the optimum time. In some circumstances, for example a fall of horse or rider or taking the course in the wrong order, elimination may occur.

The third and final phase, the jumping test, is run in reverse order with the highest placed rider following the cross-country, being the last to attempt the course of 10 to 13 obstacles. As with a normal show jumping competition, faults are awarded should a horse bring down a pole, refuse at a jump or exceed the time limit. The overall winner of the event is the rider whose combined dressage, cross-country and jumping mark is the lowest.

still run in this extended format, the majority, including the Olympic Games

Polo

History

The true origins of the sport of polo are forever lost in the mists of time. It is, however, known that a similar game called *chaughan*, meaning "mallet", was played in Persia as long as 2,000 years ago as a means of training units of cavalry. But this was not a game whose roots were confined to the Middle East. In Japan a version called *Da-Kyu* was played, in Turkey it was *Djirid* whilst on the open plains of the Russian Steppes it was called *Khis Kouhou*. For the source of the more familiar name of the sport we must look towards Tibet where it was known as *Pulu*, simply meaning "ball".

Polo has been popular in India since the 15th century and it was here, in the northern state of Manipur, that 400 years later British soldiers and tea planters witnessed the game for the first time. Taking the game to heart, a group of British cavalry officers devised a set of arbitrary rules in the 1850s and in 1862 the world's first polo club was formed at

Silchar in the west of Manipur.

In 1869 the first recorded polo match to be played on British soil took place after Edward "Chicken" Hartopp of the 10th Royal Hussars read about the sport while stationed at Aldershot. With a band of fellow officers, he organised a competition against the rival 9th Lancers on Hounslow Heath. Known then as "hockey on horseback" it quickly took off with other regiments and soon the 1st Life Guards and the Royal Horse

Guards had teams of their own.

Before long the sport was taking hold across the globe. In 1875 the first official polo match was played in Argentina where it had been taken by English and Irish engineers, many of whom were ex-military men. The following year it had reached both Australia and the United States, the latter courtesy of the great American publisher and adventurer Gordon Bennett Jr who had witnessed the game being played in England at Hurlingham and immediately took it to New York where it proved an instant success.

Polo was included at the Olympic Games for the first time in 1900 where a combined British, American and Irish team representing Hurlingham beat the British, American and Spanish team of Rugby Polo club in the final 3-1. Polo last featured as an Olympic sport at the 1936 Berlin Games by which time it was being played by true national sides. In that final Olympic outing Argentina, who were the undisputed masters of the game in what is regarded as Polo's golden age, all but annihilated Great Britain in the final 11-0 in front of a crowd of 45,000 spectators. It is estimated that polo is now played in more than 84 nations across the globe.

The Modern Game

The modern game of polo is played upon a field measuring 300yds x 200yds by two teams each consisting of four players with a ball of between 3 to 3½ inches in diameter weighing at least 3½ to 4½ ounces. Each player wears a numbered jersey denoting their area of responsibility on the field – 1 is the most forward, 4 the most defensive. By tradition the captain wears the number 3.

The field is marked with a centre line and penalty lines at 30yds, 40yds and 60yds from each goal line. At each end of the field is a goal measuring 8yds wide. The object of the game is to score goals against your opponent by striking the ball between the goal posts using a polo mallet constructed of hardwood attached to a bamboo shaft. Goals are switched after each point scored to equalise the conditions for both teams.

A match is divided into between four and six periods, known as chukkas, each lasting seven minutes in duration. A six chukka match is considered the norm in most competitions. The polo ponies, which may be of any height, are changed at the end of every chukka with no pony playing more than two chukkas in a single match. Penalties are awarded for dangerous play; however, it is permissible to ride a player off of his line or to hook the head of his mallet with your own.

Racing

History

Regardless of nationality, upbringing or background, humans are naturally competitive beings. It was, therefore, a certainty that once man first learned how to tame and ride his equine companion he would soon look to match one against another in tests of strength, endurance and speed.

Although there is evidence of ancient horse races taking place in Syria, Egypt and Babylonia it remains unclear when exactly the first formal horse races were held although a series of clay tablets dating from 1,400 BC and relating to the training of horses for racing were excavated in Cappadocia (now part of Turkey). Whilst chariot races were introduced to the Olympic Games in 664 BC it was not until 624 BC and the 33rd Olympiad that a race for mounted horses was held and another 50 years until saddled horses were competed.

The earliest documented horse race in England took place at Netherby in North Yorkshire in about 210 AD between Arabian horses brought to the country by the forces of Roman Emperor Severus Alexander. By the reign of Richard I (1157–1199) the horse race was a popular and fashionable pastime for the knights and barons but it was only in 1540 during the reign of Henry VIII that the first permanent course was officially constructed at Roodee near Chester where it exists to this day.

In around 1750 The Jockey Club was formed by a group of gentlemen who shared a passion for the sport. Originally meeting at the Star & Garter pub on London's Pall Mall it was soon relocated to the Suffolk town of Newmarket where it still remains. The set of rules devised by the club for the management and fair running of their own races on Newmarket Heath proved so popular that they were steadily adopted across the whole country and over time The Jockey Club assumed responsibility for all horse racing on British shores.

Newmarket was also an important part of the development of horse racing in the United States although in its case it was the Newmarket of New York's Long Island; the location of the

continent's first officially organised race in 1665 by Governor Richard Nicholls.

The Modern Competition

The three principal forms of horse racing contested in the United Kingdom are Flat Racing, National Hunt and Point-to-Point.

Flat Racing is, as the name suggests, a race over a predetermined distance of between 5 furlongs and 2 miles which, unlike National Hunt and Point-to-Point, does not require riders to negotiate hurdles or fences. Racing takes place on either a natural grass or synthetic all-weather surface. The highest profile flat races in the United

at Aintree in the Grand National Meet.

Point-to-Point racing is an amateur form of horse racing for hunting horses. All horses in Point-to-Point races are required to be registered Thoroughbreds except in Hunt Members races. All competing horses must obtain a certificate from a Master of Foxhounds confirming that they have hunted for at least four days in that season. Point-to-Points must, with a few exceptions, be run over a distance of 3 miles and contested over birch or spruce jumps of approximately 4ft 3in in height.

In the United States racing over jumps is almost unheard of with all of the major competitions being run on the flat and usually on an all-weather or dirt surface. It is, however, the world's foremost harness racing nation. Also popular in countries such as France, Sweden, Italy and Australia, harness races are run at a specified gait with the horses pulling a lightweight two-wheeled buggy called a sulkie. In trotting races the horse moves at a standard, if somewhat speedy trot with its legs working in diagonal pairs while in a pacing race the horse works with its legs working in lateral pairs.

Kingdom are the Epsom Derby, the 2000 Guineas held at Newmarket and the St Leger held at Doncaster.

There are three types of National Hunt race; "chases" which are run of a distance of between 2 miles and 4.5 miles with fences that are a minimum of 4ft 6in tall; "hurdles" contested at between 2 miles and 3.5 miles over hurdles no smaller than 3ft 6in; National Hunt flat races run over 1.5 miles to 2.5 miles without obstacles. The most famous National Hunt races are those held at the Cheltenham Festival which includes the prestigious Gold Cup and

Endurance

History

Regarded as a true test of genuine horsemanship, the origins of Endurance riding are found not through a desire to compete but through a need to travel long distances. Ever since horses were first domesticated, the desire to own and ride a healthy, sound and reliable mount has been paramount.

The forerunners of the modern competitive endurance competitions were the demanding cavalry tests held in the late 19th and early 20th centuries by the mounted regiments of the German, French and Austro–Hungarian armies. They were originally designed to test the stamina and fitness of both horse and rider but all too often resulted in injury or worse. Only when the organisers of the 1903 Paris Deauville Military Raid imposed a speed restriction did matters start to improve.

Endurance riding as we know it owes its heritage to the phenomenal United States Mounted Service Cup

for army personnel. First held in 1919, this gruelling five-day test of man and horse started in Vermont at Fort Ethan Allen and finished at Camp Devens in Massachusetts – a total distance of 300 miles. Each horse was expected to carry a rider weighing no less than 145lbs and the complete cavalry equipment required to be carried by a United States

Cavalry soldier on field service which weighed in at an additional 100lbs.

It was not until the 1950s that the notion of Endurance riding as a competitive sport began to emerge. On 7th August 1955, inspired by stories of the old West, a 59-year-old Wendell Robie and four of his friends set out from Lake Tahoe on the California-Nevada border and headed west along the old route of the Pony Express. Within 24 hours he and his Arab stallion, Bandos, had reached their destination of the city of Auburn 100 miles away. This ride evolved into the Western States Trail Ride, now known as the Tevis Cup, and now attracts in excess of 250 competitors every year.

Endurance in its modern form arrived in Europe in the late 1960s with the Endurance Horse and Pony Society being formed in the United Kingdom in 1973. The sport finally gained the recognition it deserved in 1982 when it was approved by the sport's governing body, the FEI, as an official discipline. At that time there were just four international competitions. The first FEI Endurance World Championships were held in 1998 in the United Arab

Emirates. With competitors from 47 different nations taking part it was declared a resounding success and as a result there are now more than 300 international Endurance competitions taking place globally each year.

The Modern Competition

Even within the world of equestrianism the sport of Endurance Riding is all too frequently dismissed by those with little knowledge of what it entails. There is, however, no other equestrian sport that demands so much from both horse and rider in terms of fitness, concentration and calculated riding. Riders in the 21st century readily use energy drinks for themselves, heart rate monitors on their horses and increasingly hi-tech tack from magnesium stirrups to lightweight Kevlar bridles and saddles with carbon fibre inserts.

Competitions comprise a number of consecutive sections known as phases. A rider may choose their own pace at which to ride, in addition it is permissible to lead or be led by the horse as long as the competitor is mounted when crossing both the start and finish lines. At the end of each phase, usually no further than 25 miles there is a mandatory veterinary inspection, or "vetgate", at which the horse must be presented within a set period of time. Each horse is then examined for soundness and general wellbeing before being allowed to continue with the next phase. A final veterinary inspection is carried out at the end of the competition to ensure that horses are not ridden beyond their limits. Any horse displaying excessive fatigue or apparent lameness at any point in the competition is eliminated, otherwise known as being "vetted out".

Although there is nobody more important in an Endurance competition than a horse and its rider, their success would not be possible without the assistance of a dedicated and well drilled support crew. They will travel by motor vehicle on nearby roads and tracks and intercept their team at pre-designated locations on the course to supply water, feeds and cooling "slosh" bottles to keep both horse and jockey in tip-top condition.

Driving

History

Long before man ever took to riding horses he was using them for driving and, for that reason, driving is the oldest of all equestrian sports. Chariots were in use from at least 2,000 BC, the earliest evidence of their use being the Sintasha chariot burials on the banks of the Tobol River in Russia's Southern Ural Mountains.

The first driving competitions were the chariot races of the Mycenaeans, the Ancient Greeks and the Romans. For the Greeks it was an Olympic sport with races being held for both two- and four-horse chariots. In Rome wealthy and influential backers often paid large sums of money to secure the services of the best charioteers.

Gambling was very popular in 18th century England as was carriage driving – it was, after all, the principal form of transport for any self-respecting gentleman of means. It is, therefore, no surprise that the speed, stamina and skill of a driver and his horses were a common subject for an informal wager. This enthusiasm for driving led to the formation of driving clubs, the membership of which was seen as highly fashionable.

Modern Competition

Horse driving remains a skilled and highly competitive sport to this day and is enjoyed at many different levels. Scurry racing, an incredibly fast moving and exciting sport contested by teams of

ponies around tight, twisting courses at breakneck speed, is immensely popular at events such as the Horse of the Year Show. The precision and control is often hard to believe as teams thunder between markers barely inches wider than the scurry carriage itself.

At the other end of the scale is the sport of Combined Driving or Horse Driving Trials. Contested by single horse combinations, in pairs or, the most impressive of all, as a four-in-hand, they are run on a similar format to a three-day event. Teams are first required to complete a dressage routine of compulsory figures within the confines of a 100m x 40m arena where, as with a ridden dressage competition, marks are awarded for obedience, smoothness of transition, impulsion and paces. There follows what is known as "The Marathon" – the driving equivalent of an eventing cross-country. Teams must complete a course of up to 22km whilst negotiating seemingly impossible turns, water obstacles, steep climbs and rough terrain. Finally the teams are faced with an Obstacle Driving test in which drivers must weave a clean line through a narrow track marked by cones upon which marker balls have been balanced.

Hunting

Although man has hunted on horseback for thousands of years, it was not until the 17th century that the sport of fox hunting was introduced to Britain. Records suggest that England's oldest hunt is the Bilsdale which was established in 1668 by George Villiers, Duke of Buckingham, at Helmsley Castle in North Yorkshire.

Early hunts were slow and inefficient affairs – their hounds being bred for scent rather than for pace. However, by the end of the 18th century a great deal had changed; the influence of the Thoroughbred meant that horses were getting faster and hounds too were now being bred for speed and stamina. The landscape had changed too with the enforcement of the Inclosure Acts that saw once open countryside divided and fenced.

The years of the 19th century are seen by many as the halcyon days of fox hunting in Britain. In a landscape unscarred by busy, traffic-filled roads, intense farming and restrictive practices

the countryside was truly the hunting field's playground.

Since the introduction of the Hunting Act 2004, hunting with hounds has effectively been banned in England and Wales – a ban had been enforced in Scotland since 2002. Despite this, the majority of the 184 hunts registered with the Master of Foxhounds Association continue to operate

following artificially laid trails.

Hunts are highly organised affairs; each one being headed up by a Master of Foxhounds (MFH) who has overall responsibility for its smooth running and the employment of its staff (known as servants). These are the Huntsmen and Whippers-in who manage the hounds in the field, the Kennelsmen who look after the hounds in the hunt kennels and the Terriermen who look after and control the hunt's terriers.

Despite the impression often given to the contrary, it is only members of the hunt staff and invited members who wear the scarlet hunt coats, known as pinks, whilst in the field. Even the wearing of hunt buttons is restricted to those given suitable permission. The remaining members are to be found in navy or black.

Working Horses

Police Horses

To this day, police horses are employed by forces in major cities across the world. Highly visible and somewhat imposing they are proven to be a valuable asset in situations of crowd control where they offer their rider an unparalleled elevated view.

Horses used by the London Metropolitan Police Mounted Branch undergo six months of training which is broken down into three phases known as red, amber and green. At the red stage horses are taught basic manners and made familiar with the day to day tasks of loading and unloading. They then move on to the amber stage during which they are introduced to new environments, familiarised with mounted police equipment and taught to stand quietly. In the final green stage horses patrol for up to two hours each day and are introduced to the heavy congested traffic of the nation's capital. They also receive specialised training at the force's Public Order Training Centre in Gravesend, are taught to patrol in the dark, and are even introduced to the noise and fervour of military bands!

In addition to providing an essential service to the police in their fight against crime, they also act as a wonderful means of breaking down barriers with the public. There are very few police horses that would not enjoy a gentle pat on the neck or a mint to crunch on.

Military Horses

For centuries the horse played a crucial role in the structure, tactics and success of armies across the world. A staggering 30,000 cavalry took to the battlefield at Waterloo in 1815 and in excess of 1.5 million horses were pressed into service during the First World War. Thankfully the days of massed regiments of cavalry charging into battle on horseback are now consigned to the past although horses do still play an important, albeit ceremonial role, in the modern day army.

Based in London at the Hyde Park Barracks, the Household Cavalry Mounted Regiment is as much one of the capital's landmarks as the double-decker bus, Nelson's Column or Buckingham Palace. Comprising two squadrons – the Blues & Royals and the Life Guards – it is the Queen's official escort on State occasions. Only black horses are used by the regiment with the exception of the greys ridden by the State Trumpeters and the usually coloured heavy drum horses. Whilst highly skilled horsemen, every member of the Mounted Regiment is also a fully trained regular soldier and can be called into action on the frontline.

American
Quarter Horse

Described as a horse that could "turn on a dime and toss you back nine cents in change", the Quarter Horse is often seen as one of the original building blocks that helped create the United States of America.

The first truly American breed, it originated from the nation's eastern seaboard in the early 1600s when imported English horses were crossed

American Quarter Horse	
Place of Origin	United States
Average Height	14.3–16.1hh
Colour	Usually chestnut but can be any solid colour
Other Names	–
Uses	General riding, cattle, polo, racing, rodeo

with "native" types of Iberian and Arabian descent brought to the continent by the Spanish Conquistadors a century earlier. Put to work on farms, in harness and as a riding horse, the breed soon developed into a compact, stocky and well muscled type that not only possessed considerable endurance but also displayed an incredible turn of speed over shorter distances. Often put to test in sprint races held at local fairs, this working-man's racehorse soon became known simply as the Quarter Horse after the distance – a quarter of a mile – at which it excelled.

With the opening of the west, the Quarter Horse proved to be the ideal mount and companion for the pioneering settlers – its natural agility, balance and pace and its innate ability to work with cattle making it the perfect cow-herding pony.

The popularity of the American Quarter Horse continues to this day with over three million examples registered worldwide. Whilst most live relatively sedate lives as riding ponies, many still earn their keep working on ranches across the country whilst others are put through their paces at rodeos.

Fun Facts

The American Quarter Horse is sometimes referred to as "America's fastest athlete" – reputedly capable of travelling at over 50mph in short bursts, it is easy to understand why!

Andalusian

The dramatic, powerful Andalusian with its high crest and extravagant paces is one of the world's oldest and most revered horse breeds.

Correctly known since 1912 as the *Pura Raza Española* (abbreviated to PRE), the purebred Spanish Horse can trace its ancestry back to the ancient Sorraia ponies which roamed the country's vast plains in great numbers during pre-Christian times. Interbreeding with imported Barb and other North African types created a faster, more enduring horse which, with the Roman occupation of the Iberian Peninsula, was soon recognised for its worth as a military mount. Stud farms were quickly established in southern Spain in Baetica (today's Andalusia) to

Andalusian	
Place of Origin	Spain
Average Height	15.2hh
Colour	Usually grey but also black, bay and chestnut
Other Names	Purebred Spanish Horse (PRE)
Uses	Dressage, show jumping, bullfighting

Fun Facts

The Andalusian's stunning looks and inherent ability to be trained has made it a popular choice for use in film and has been seen in productions from Raiders of the Lost Ark to Lord of the Rings.

provide cavalry horses to the Empire's northern provinces.

Strong, compact and naturally agile, the breed became a logical participant in the national sport of bullfighting. However, since the time of the Renaissance the Andalusian has also excelled at *Haute École* – the highest level of dressage famed for its "airs above the ground". Whilst in modern times these grand manoeuvres may be confined to the demonstrations of the elite Cadre Noir and the Real Escuela Andaluza, the Andalusian continues to prove its worth in dressage competitions across the world right up to Grand Prix level.

Anglo-Arab

With its impressive speed, stamina, scope and levelheadedness the Anglo-Arab is often considered the perfect sporting all-rounder. A product of crossing the Thoroughbred and the Arab, there is a common misconception that the breed originated in England when, in fact, it is of early 19th century French origin. In France the Thoroughbred is known as the *Pur Sang Anglais,* whilst the Arabian is the *Pur Sang Arabe* – the cross of the two being the *Anglais-Arabe,* or Anglo-Arab as it soon became known.

For many years the centres of Anglo-Arab breeding were the studs of Pau, Tarbes, Gelos and, most importantly, the national stud at Château Pompadour from where director Eugène Gayot set up a systematic programme of breeding in 1836 based upon two Arab stallions, Aslan and Massoud, and three imported English Thoroughbreds, Daer, Commus Mare and Selim Mare.

The precise requirements for Anglo-Arab registration vary from

Fun Facts

Many of the first Anglo-Arabs registered in the SBF (Stud Book Français) have ancestry traceable to registered Arabians imported to France from Egypt in the early 1800s by Napoleon Bonaparte.

nation to nation but, as a rule, to be entered into the studbook a horse must possess a minimum of 25 per cent and a maximum of 75 per cent Arab blood with only Arab, Thoroughbred or Anglo-Arab bloodlines.

By taking the best aspects of its ancestry, the Anglo-Arab's balanced temperament, jumping ability and endurance have earned it a reputation as a formidable eventer.

Anglo-Arab	
Place of Origin	France
Average Height	15.3–16.3hh
Colour	Chestnut, bay or brown
Other Names	-
Uses	Eventing, show jumping, hunting

Appaloosa

The distinctive Appaloosa is one of those breeds whose precise origins are less than clear. There is evidence of the existence of spotted horses amongst the cave paintings of Peche Merle and Lascaux in France that dates back over 20,000 years. However, the Appaloosa, as we know it, is of North American origin.

Several theories exist as to how the spotted horses first made their way to the Americas. The most common

Appaloosa	
Place of Origin	United States
Average Height	14.2–15.2hh
Colour	Coloured with spotting
Other Names	Palouse Horse
Uses	General riding, jumping, racing

and, indeed, most probable is that they accompanied the Spanish Conquistadors in the 15th and 16th centuries; others believe that they were brought across by Russian fur traders. It is also thought that they may have arrived as late as the turn of the 19th century, traded to the Spanish settlers on the West Coast.

It was, however, the people of the Nez Perce – a nomadic tribe

who lived in what is now Oregon, Washington and Idaho – who were responsible for making the breed what it is today. Fearsome warriors, expert horsemen and knowledgeable breeders, they concentrated on developing the desirable qualities of endurance, intelligence and temperament whilst retaining its individual appearance. Pressure from the US Government on the tribe to relinquish its land unfortunately resulted in the Nez Perce War of 1877 which saw the herds dispersed by the US Cavalry through sales and slaughter leaving the breed all but extinct.

There was, however, resurgence in interest during the late 1930s after an article in the *Western Horseman* journal highlighted the breed's unique characteristics. Since then the breed has recovered to become one of the most popular in the United States today as well as finding favour overseas.

Fun Facts

In the 1930s the Appaloosa was referred to as a "Palouse Horse" after the Palouse River that ran through Nez Perce country. This evolved first to "Palousey" then to "Appalousey" and finally "Appaloosa".

Arab

The Arab is universally accepted as the oldest and purest of all the world's horse breeds. Originating, as its name suggests, from the Middle East, it was the preferred mount for the tribesmen of the Bedouin who used its pace and stamina to travel great distances over the harsh and arid desert landscape at speed with little need for food or water and without fear of becoming unsound. Bedouin tribesmen favoured using mares over stallions for their raiding parties as they were easier to keep quiet. The Bedouin legacy lives on to this day in the world of competitive endurance riding where the Arab breed is dominant.

Gentle by nature and unmistakable in appearance thanks to the unique and distinctive shape of its head, the Arab is seen by many as one of the most beautiful of all horse breeds. Standing, on average, at just 15hh and without excessive bone, it is a deceptively strong breed and is capable of carrying a disproportionately heavy amount of weight for its size.

Above all other breeds, the Arab has exercised a phenomenal influence on the development of the world's equine

Arab	
Place of Origin	Middle East
Average Height	14.1-15.1hh
Colour	Chestnut, grey, bay, black
Other Names	Arabian
Uses	Endurance, showing

Fun Facts
Emperor Napoleon Bonaparte was an enormous fan of the purebred Arab; his favourite being the impressive grey stallion Marengo upon whom he commanded his forces at Waterloo. Marengo lived to the grand old age of 38 and his preserved skeleton is now on public display at the National Army Museum in Chelsea, London.

population – its bloodlines having frequently been introduced into other breeds in an attempt to increase stamina and soundness. Most significantly it was intrinsic in the creation of the Thoroughbred in the 18th century.

Ardennais

The mighty Ardennais is possibly the oldest of all heavy horse breeds with a history dating back over 2000 years. Although its precise origins are the subject of debate, it is thought that it is descended from the ancient horses of Solutré. Praised by Julius Caesar in his *De Bello Gallico* and subsequently by Napoleon, the Ardennais has for many centuries worked the land of the Ardennes Plateau by the banks of the Meuse on the borders of France, Belgium and Luxembourg.

For a great deal of its existence the Ardennais was a smaller beast than is seen today and was often to be found under saddle or in harness. Only with the turn of the 19th century were alternative bloodlines intentionally introduced including those from the Arab, the powerful Percheron and the Belgian Draught. This has resulted in the creation of three different types – the original smaller Ardennais which still survives in small numbers, the more common Trait du Nord and the massive Auxois.

Incredibly, despite their enormity – weighing in at anything up to 1,000kg – the Ardennais in all of its derivatives remains a calm, tolerant and docile creature known for its gentleness and unparalleled ease of handling.

Ardennais	
Place of Origin	Belgium & France
Average Height	15-16.2hh
Colour	Grey, roan, chestnut, bay
Other Names	Trait du Nord, Auxois
Uses	Draught

Fun Facts

From the time of Napoleon through until the end of the First World War the Ardennais were considered to be the best artillery horses in the whole of Europe.

Barb

While it is undisputable that, over the centuries, the horse has played a crucial role in the history of man, there are still very few breeds that can claim to have conquered a nation.

For over 200 years the Iberian Peninsula had been controlled by the Visigoths – a warlike people responsible for the fall of Rome in 410 AD. Heavily armoured and with a taste for battle they had seemed

all but invincible. That was until the arrival in the early 8th century of an invading Arab-Berber army from North Africa that was light and mobile and mounted on exceptionally fast, nimble and responsive horses known as Barbs that could run rings around their overweight opponents.

Riders of the strong and intelligent Barb had created a style of horsemanship that would become known as *jineta* after the Zanata Berber tribe. This required the rider to adopt a bent knee position in short stirrups and utilise a bridle with a strong bit and curb chain. To this the horse would respond by working through the neck allowing very tight turns and razor sharp braking.

In addition to performing a key role in the development of the Andalusian

Barb	
Place of Origin	Morocco
Average Height	14.2-15.2hh
Colour	Bay, dark bay, black, grey
Other Names	Berber Horse, Barbary Horse
Uses	General riding

horse, the Barb has also played an influential part in the advancement of many other breeds including the Thoroughbred and Anglo-Arab. Sadly, with the breed being considered less attractive than its Arab cousin it has always failed to receive the same level of recognition and accolade.

Belgian Draught

This ancient breed is thought to be directly descended from the mighty Ardennais and is often known as the Brabant after the historic region of the Low Countries from where it originated. By the mid-19th century three distinct types of Belgian horse had become recognised based not on conformational differences but primarily on bloodline and size – the *Gros de la Dendre*, the *Colosses de la Mehaigne* and the *Gris de Nivelles et du Hainaut*. Although several other smaller studbooks had previously been created, it was not until 1885 that five highly influential breeders started the official Studbook of the Belgian Draught.

Large, powerful, quick to learn and willing to work, these leviathans were ideal for heavy draught work and were the heavy agricultural tractors of their day. In 1903 the Belgian government sent several examples of the breed, first to the International Livestock Exposition in Chicago and then on to

Fun Facts

One of the Belgian Draught's predecessors – the Flanders Horse – was instrumental in the creation of the mighty Clydesdale and Suffolk Punch.

the famous 1904 St Louis World Fair. The Belgian Draught generated a great deal of interest and many horses were exported to the United States until the outbreak of the First World War.

With the increased use of mechanised farming methods, the importance of the Belgian Draught as a working horse waned following the Second World War leaving the breed in danger of extinction. However, recent years have seen a welcome resurgence of interest in the breed for showing.

Belgian Draught	
Place of Origin	Spain
Average Height	16.2-17hh
Colour	Chestnut, roan, bay, dun, grey
Other Names	Brabant, Brabançon, Flanders Horse
Uses	Draught

Boulonnais

Always regarded as one of the most beautiful of all the world's draught breeds, the spectacular Boulonnais can trace its earliest origins back to the interbreeding between native mares of northern France and fiery stallions of the Roman army as Caesar's forces prepared to invade Britain in 55 BC. The basis of the breed, however, started to come into its own during the time of the Crusades thanks to the input of two knowledgeable breeders – Eustache, Comte de Boulogne and Robert, Comte d'Artois – who crossed this local stock with Mecklenbergs from Germany to create a horse that was fast and agile but more than capable of carrying a heavily armoured knight into battle.

The Spanish occupation of Flanders in the 17th century saw the introduction of Andalusian, Barb and Arabian blood into the breed and the now characteristic look and graceful movement of the wonderful Boulonnais emerged.

By the 18th century two distinct types of Boulonnais had developed: the *Maree*, which we recognise today, and the smaller, faster *Mareyeur* or Horse of the Tide – so called because it was utilised to transport heavy carts of fish from Boulogne to Paris, a distance of over 200

Boulonnais	
Place of Origin	Northern France
Average Height	15.3–17hh
Colour	Grey
Other Names	White Marble Horse
Uses	Draught

Fun Facts

The astounding exploits of the Mareyeur are celebrated each year with the running of the Route du Poisson – a 300km 22-stage relay race in which each team of 10 pairs of horses vies to be first to bring a basket of fish from Boulogne to Chantilly.

miles, in less than 18 hours.

At the height of its popularity there were in excess of 600,000 Boulonnais horses in northern France, however, after the region was ravaged by two World Wars, and the tractor took over as the principal source of agricultural pulling power, the numbers have dwindled dramatically – at present there are thought to be fewer than 1,000 in Europe.

Breton

As its name suggests, the Breton horse originates from the northwestern French province of Bretagne (Brittany). Bred locally for many hundreds of years it has become renowned for its remarkable strength, durability and hardiness.

As with many of the larger breeds, it became increasingly popular during the

Middle Ages with knights preparing for their arduous Crusades in the Middle East. The Breton, in particular, was revered for its gentle movement and comfortable gait – admirable qualities when many long hours in the saddle wearing full armour are a prospect. Through the ages the Breton was frequently crossbred with other heavy draught breeds, but its distinctive small trot, willing nature and flaxen mane have been retained.

Three types of Breton exist today, each having been bred to perform a specific task. The Heavy Draught Breton, developed by crossing with the Percheron and Ardennais, is the most powerful and, at over 16hh, the largest of the three, whilst the Postier Breton, created during the 19th century by crossbreeding with the Norfolk Trotter and the Hackney is finer, has a striking gait and makes an admirable carriage horse. The last of the three, the Corlay Breton, is really the true descendent of the original native horses. At just 14.3-15hh it is a more compact animal and is, like its ancestors, the best suited to the harder conditions of life on the Atlantic coast but can also make a fine riding horse.

Breton	
Place of Origin	Brittany, France
Average Height	14.3-16hh
Colour	Roan, chestnut, grey
Other Names	-
Uses	Draught, driving, general riding

Camargue

Born black or brown before turning grey in maturity, the Camargue horse is today one of the world's most strictly controlled breeds. Resident of a triangular area of southern France bordered by Tarascon-sur-Rhône to the north, Fos-sur-Mer to the east and Montpellier to the west and incorporating the Ile de Camargue,

the plains of Heacuterault and parts of the Crau, the breed has existed since prehistoric times from when, some say, it could well have been related to the famous but now extinct Soutré horse.

With the passing of the centuries the breed has been influenced by other types of horse brought with the countless armies that have passed through the region including those of the Greeks, the Romans and the Goths.

Subjected to extremes of weather from scorching Mediterranean heat to icy Alpine winds, the resilient horses of the Camargue live wild in the marshland of the Parc Naturel Régional de Camargue in small herds consisting of a single stallion, his mares and their offspring. Breeding is wild but maintained under the auspices of the staff of a conservation research station at la Tour du Valat.

Fun Facts

Due to its natural coastal habitat on the Mediterranean coast, the Camargue horse is also known romantically as the White Horse of the Sea.

Despite its lively nature and wild origins, the Camargue horse has proved to be a willing and able riding horse and is used by the region's own cowboys, the *Gardiano*, in the management of the famous Camargue bull herd, as well as providing visitors to the area with a unique way of exploring the park.

Camargue

Place of Origin	Southern France
Average Height	13.1–14.1hh
Colour	White
Other Names	Horse of the Sea
Uses	Cattle herding, general riding

Cleveland Bay

The stunning Cleveland Bay is the oldest of Britain's native horse breeds. Its direct ancestor was the Chapman horse – a breed so called because it was used extensively by chapmen, the travelling salesmen of the day, to carry their wares from village to village. The Chapman was a remarkable all-rounder capable not only of packhorse duties but also for general riding, carriage driving and even light farm work.

To this strong foundation Spanish blood was added in the latter part of the 17th century – Andalusian horses being widespread in the North East of the country following the English Civil War. There were also strong trading links between the region's principal seaport, Whitby, and those of the North African coast which, in turn, saw the introduction of the Barb to the area and to the bloodlines.

With time the breed developed into the handsome creature that we see today before reaching a peak in its popularity in the late 19th century when the

Cleveland Bay	
Place of Origin	Yorkshire, England
Average Height	16-16.2hh
Colour	Bay with black legs, mane and tail
Other Names	Chapman Horse (no longer used)
Uses	Hunting, driving

Fun Facts

The Cleveland Bay has become somewhat of a royal favourite with several examples in service at the Royal Mews. Queen Elizabeth II herself is the patron of the Cleveland Bay Horse Society whilst her husband, Prince Philip, has previously favoured the breed when competing at four-in-hand carriage driving.

Cleveland Bay Horse Society of Great Britain was formed and its first studbook published in 1884. But, despite its classic looks and undeniable versatility, the breed started to fade with the advent of the motor car and mechanised farming with even more being lost to the First World War battlefields of northern France and Belgium where it was heavily utilised as an artillery horse.

By the turn of the 1960s just five mature Cleveland Bay stallions were known to exist. However, thanks to the tireless and diligent efforts of a dedicated band of admirers the breed has undergone a spectacular resurgence in popularity and, whilst actual numbers may still be relatively small, its status as an endangered breed is no longer a concern.

Clydesdale

First developed by the farmers of Lanarkshire on the banks of the River Clyde just over 200 years ago, the impressive Clydesdale is far from being an ancient breed when compared with the Arab or the Barb. However, like its North African cousins, it is certainly one of the most recognised and loved.

It was originally bred not only to work the agricultural land of the Scots farmers but to provide heavy haulage for the Lanarkshire coalfields and in the industrial centre of Glasgow. Over the years its reputation as an easy to manage,

willing and hard worker has earned it respect the world over and examples can be found still working across the globe.

Despite weighing in at over a tonne and standing as tall as 18hh, the Clydesdale has an athletic appearance and is less heavily proportioned than many of its other draught relatives such as the Percheron or the Suffolk Punch allowing it to move with surprisingly elegant paces.

The Clydesdale's calm, unflappable nature and impressive weight-carrying ability has seen it used for many years as a ceremonial drum horse in events such as the Trooping of the Colour and the Edinburgh Tattoo. The Household Cavalry's current drum horse, Spartacus, is a Clydesdale cross.

Fun Facts

One of the world's largest herds of Clydesdales is owned by the American brewer Anheuser-Busch. The Budweiser Clydesdales work in teams of eight to pull an ale delivery wagon complete with two drivers and two Dalmatian dogs!

Clydesdale	
Place of Origin	Scotland
Average Height	16–18hh
Colour	Bay, brown, grey, black, roan
Other Names	-
Uses	Draught, drum horse

Connemara

I reland's only remaining indigenous breed, the Connemara pony is named after the barren and mountainous region in the west of the country from where the breed is thought to have originated. Covered in seemingly endless peat bogs and moorland, this harsh environment has helped shape a hardy and agile breed with an impressive ability to jump that defies its diminutive stature.

The Connemara's roots probably trace back to the mounts of Celtic warriors who came to Ireland over 2,500 years ago. Links have also been suggested that connect the breed to the now extinct Irish Hobby that was common in the British Isles prior to the 13th century. However, legend tells that

Connemara	
Place of Origin	Ireland
Average Height	14-14.2hh
Colour	Grey, black, dun, bay, brown
Other Names	-
Uses	Showing, jumping, general riding

Fun Facts

Cannonball, the first stallion to be entered in the Connemara studbook was the outright winner of the Oughterard Farmers' Race for 16 successive years. What was the secret of his success? The night before the race this grey would devour half a barrel of oats!

an amount of Iberian blood was infused into the breed in the 16th century after fleeing ships of the Spanish Armada sank in storms off of the Connemara coast and some surviving horses swam ashore and bred with the native stock.

Fearless over jumps, fast in open country and a nimble mover, there are very few breeds of pony that can claim to the all round sporting abilities of the Connemara and for that reason it has become the mount of choice for many young, up-and-coming riders, whilst crossed with the Thoroughbred it can make for an ideal senior competition horse.

Criollo

The Criollo is the result of many years selective breeding of the *baguales*, a feral horse found exclusively in the Pampas region of Argentina where it now enjoys the status of being the country's national horse.

The *baguales'* origin can be found in the elegant Spanish horses brought to the Americas by the Conquistadors in the 16th century. Over the years many horses escaped or were abandoned and it did not take long for these to form together to create feral herds. The Argentinean Pampas, a far stretching area of fertile open grassland covering over 250,000 square miles, proved to be their ideal habitat.

However, as time passed the agricultural worth of the Pampas became apparent to the country's pioneering settlers and soon the area became zigzagged with enclosure fences, crops and farm livestock. Only in 1917 was action finally taken to protect and preserve Argentina's "native" horse with the formation of the Sociedad Rural de Argentina who located a herd of 200 that had been cared for by native Indians and used them as a foundation to maintain and

Criollo	
Place of Origin	Argentina
Average Height	15hh
Colour	All colours
Other Names	-
Uses	Cattle herding, polo

Fun Facts

In Argentina each year the Criollo Breeders Association organises an endurance ride for purebred Criollo horses. Lasting 14 days and covering 465 miles it must be completed in less than 75 hours. The minimum weight for rider and tack is 100kg whilst the only food permitted is that found naturally along the trail.

rebuild the breed. At first the horse was known as the Argentinean before its name was changed to the now familiar Criollo, or Creole.

The Criollo is best known as the pony of the *Gauchos* – Argentina's legendary cowboys who look after the vast nation's vast herds of beef cattle. Its bloodlines have, however, spread far and wide across the globe as when crossed with the Thoroughbred it can produce the fast, agile and fearless Polo Pony.

Dales Pony

If a Thoroughbred were to be described as the Jaguar or Aston Martin of the horse world then the fabulous Dales Pony could only be likened to the trusty Land Rover. A product of the harsh environment of the eastern Pennines it was once the powerhouse that kept the lead mines of the Yorkshire Dales functioning. Standing no taller than 14.2hh it was not only put to work underground but was also used to haul enormous 100kg packs containing pigs of lead from the mines to the ports on the North East coast before returning with equally heavy packs of supplies and coal.

The Dales Pony was also noted for its outstanding trotting ability both in saddle and in harness – a skill that was added to in the 19th century with an influx of blood from the Welsh Cob.

Unsurprisingly considering its strength and ability to work in adverse conditions, the Dales Pony was pressed into service with the army during both the First and Second World Wars. But their popularity with the armed forces meant that in the peace that followed, numbers of the breed had fallen to a catastrophic low – according to records in 1955 only four filly foals were registered.

Happily, the Dales Pony's fortunes proved to be as strong as its constitution and, with the help of a dedicated band of enthusiasts, over the years the breed has experienced a good recovery and, despite being classed as a rare breed, is no longer seen as being in danger of extinction.

Dales Pony	
Place of Origin	Yorkshire Dales, England
Average Height	14.2hh
Colour	Black
Other Names	–
Uses	General riding, driving

Fun Facts

The official army specification for a Dales Pony stated that it should be over 14hh but no more than 14.2hh, not under 5 years, weighing half a tonne, with a 68in girth, and able to carry 21 stones on a mountain.

Dartmoor

The robust Dartmoor Pony is another of Britain's ancient equines. First mentioned in the will of Aelfwold, the Saxon Bishop of Crediton, in the year 1012, the breed has undergone a great deal of change in both appearance and use over the centuries.

In medieval times wheeled transport was almost unheard of on the moorland and rugged slopes of Dartmoor so it was the task of the trusty pack pony to ensure that goods and supplies were transported about the region. For many years the Dartmoor Pony was used for hauling tin from the countless mines of the region to the local stannary towns whilst in the 1800s ponies were utilised to pull heavy granite wagons on the railway from Haytor down to the quayside at Teigngrace. Strong of back and sure of foot the tough Dartmoor

Ponies served the purpose well.

From the second half of the 20th century, mechanisation saw the commercial use of the Dartmoor fall into decline with numbers of ponies on the moor dropping from 30,000 in 1950 to just 3,000 today. These ponies live a seemingly wild life being left to wander the moors at will in small herds. They are, however, all privately owned by local farmers and are given veterinary checks twice a year in mass round-ups called drifts.

Dartmoors make exceptional riding ponies having an elegant and smooth action, an even temperament and generally being ready and willing to accept training. They are highly popular in Europe especially when crossed with Arab or Thoroughbred blood.

Fun Facts

Prince Edward, later to become Edward VIII, was a frequent visitor to Dartmoor in the 1920s. He owned and bred Dartmoor Ponies at Princetown often crossing them with Arabs to produce polo ponies.

Dartmoor	
Place of Origin	Dartmoor, England
Average Height	12.2hh
Colour	Bay, black, brown
Other Names	-
Uses	General riding, jumping, hunting, showing

Dutch Warmblood

The modern Dutch Warmblood is a superb competition horse developed through the selective breeding of English, French and German horses crossed with native Dutch types. The origins of the breed can be found amongst two provinces of Holland: the centrally located Gelderland and the northerly Groningen.

For many years the breeders of Gelderland had produced a quality carriage horse that was also suitable for light draught work and riding – the Gelderlander. Their Groningen neighbours, meanwhile, developed a heavier horse derived from Oldenburg and Friesian bloodlines that was more suited to coping with the heavy clay soil of the region. Unsurprisingly, it was only a matter of time before the two breeds were put together to produce a fine middleweight all-rounder.

With the intention of improving the breed's sporting credentials Thoroughbred blood was introduced, as well as that from Holsteiners and Hanoverians, to produce what we now know as the

Dutch Warmblood	
Place of Origin	Holland
Average Height	16-16.3hh
Colour	Any colour but bay and brown are most common
Other Names	KWPN
Uses	Dressage, jumping, eventing

Fun Facts

One of the greatest Dutch Warmbloods of all time was the charismatic show jumper Milton: a stunning 16.2hh grey gelding which, ridden by John Whitaker, became the first horse outside of the racing world to win more than £1million in prize money.

Dutch Warmblood or KWPN (from Koninklijk Warmbloed Paardenstamboek Nederland – the Royal Warmblood Studbook of the Netherlands).

Demonstrating character, soundness and athleticism, in recent years the Dutch Warmblood has proved to be a top-class performance horse that can excel at the highest level in the dressage and show jumping arenas.

Exmoor Pony

many of the indigenous breeds have been changed beyond recognition by the intentional introduction of other bloodlines to create horses and ponies to suit a particular purpose.

Fortunately for the Exmoor Pony this has not been the case. For many years Exmoor was designated a Royal Forest – a hunting ground – and, with no local industry or significant agriculture to speak of, the land and the ponies were left well alone. This might all have changed when, in 1818, the Royal Forest was sold and its stock dispersed. However, Sir Thomas Acland who had been warden of the estate

Fun Facts

Bowing to its wild heritage, the Exmoor's head is larger than other breeds of comparable size – its extra-long nasal passages allowing the cold moorland air to be warmed before entering the lungs.

Wild ponies have wandered the moors and dales of Britain's wilder corners for many centuries – the first arriving somewhere between 100,000 and 200,000 years ago across the land bridge that would eventually become the English Channel. Over the years

acquired 30 ponies while several of the local farmers bought stock from local sales and continued to breed the Exmoor true to type.

The Second World War proved to be a tough time for the breed. Exmoor itself was transformed into a military training area and many of the ponies found themselves being used illicitly as live targets whilst many others were stolen and taken away to the cities to be used for meat. By the end of hostilities a mere 50 ponies survived.

Numbers gradually recovered, thanks in no small part to the efforts of local stalwart Mary Etherington who galvanised the efforts of local farmers and landowners, and now the Exmoor can be found living in healthy numbers across the country. Numbers of the breed living wild in the National Park remain steady at about 200.

Exmoor Pony	
Place of Origin	Exmoor, England
Average Height	12.3hh
Colour	Bay, brown, dun – all with black points
Other Names	-
Uses	General riding

Falabella

Despite its diminutive stature – the breed stands no taller than 30 inches when fully grown – the tiny Falabella is not a pony but a miniature horse. Bred for over 150 years on the Recreo de Rocha Ranch near Buenos Aires, Argentina, it was created by an Irishman, Patrick Newtall, after he discovered some unusually small horses amongst the Criollos of the local Indians.

Newtall acquired some stock of these smaller horses and created a miniature herd which, in 1879, he transferred to his son-in-law, Juan Falabella who, in turn, took to experimenting with the type by adding bloodlines from other breeds including small Thoroughbreds, local Criollos and imported Shetlands. Breeding continued on the Falabella's ranch with each successive generation striving to develop and perfect the attractive miniature breed.

After the Establecimientos Falabella – now called the Asociación de Criadores de Caballos Falabella or Falabella Horse Breeders Association – was established in the early 1940s by Julio Cesar Falabella, international interest in the breed started to grow and by the 1950s examples were being exported the world over.

Whilst the engaging and intelligent little Falabella is far too small for riding of any description it can make for a wonderful, if slightly unusual pet.

Falabella	
Place of Origin	Argentina
Average Height	30in maximum
Colour	Bay, black, brown, coloured, spotted
Other Names	-
Uses	Showing, in harness

Fell Pony

Ponies like the Fell and its ancestral geographic neighbour, the Dales, have existed in the North of England for many centuries. Utilised for their weight-carrying abilities from Roman times until the early 20th century, they were, for countless years, the ultimate off-road hauliers of their time.

Both the Fell and the Dales share the same genetic origins – most probably from ancient Celtic ponies – to which blood from other breeds was later added, including that of the Friesian, at one time prevalent in the area having been widely used as a light cavalry mount by the occupying Roman forces, and the Galloway. This now extinct breed was favoured by Scots raiders who needed a horse of great speed, strength and sure-footedness to negotiate the barren and hostile landscape of the border territories – all attributes which, despite the passage of time, are present in the Fell Pony.

Lighter but no less robust than its Dales cousin, the Fell proved not only to be an excellent pack animal but also to be an impressive riding horse, displaying a fantastic trot and superb stamina. As a result it was often to be found under saddle and in harness.

Modern examples can be found competing in many forms of equestrian sport. The Duke of Edinburgh, for example, competes a team of Fell

Fell Pony	
Place of Origin	North West England
Average Height	13.3-14hh
Colour	Bay, black, brown, grey
Other Names	-
Uses	General riding, driving

Fun Facts

The characteristic blue horn of the Fell Pony's hooves is inherited from its Galloway ancestors.

Ponies owned by Queen Elizabeth in carriage driving events while Fell crosses have been seen to compete well in cross-country and endurance classes.

Friesian

It seems incredible in this day and age that the magnificent Friesian was once considered to be rather ugly! That was the opinion of the Romans who, whilst acknowledging its abilities as a powerful and willing worker and a fine cavalry mount, felt nothing for its dramatic appearance.

It is, however, true that the breed's look has changed considerably over the centuries. Originating in the northern Dutch kingdom of Friesland on the North Sea coast, the Friesian was much favoured by Germanic knights bound for the crusades. They appreciated its ability to carry a fully armoured rider whilst moving with speed and agility on the battlefield.

An influx of Andalusian blood

during the Spanish occupation of the Low Countries during the Eighty Years' War helped improve the breed further – the Iberian influence extending to the Friesian's now characteristic arched neck, small head and high knee action – factors which soon endeared it to the continent's top schools of classical equitation.

While the Friesian, with its level temperament and energetic free-flowing paces remains, without a doubt, one of the world's finest riding horses, it is in harness that it truly excels – there can be few sights more thrilling than a team of shimmering Friesians at work ahead of a meticulously prepared carriage!

Friesian	
Place of Origin	Netherlands
Average Height	15hh
Colour	Black
Other Names	-
Uses	General riding, driving, dressage

Hackney

Although the modern Hackney is a product of the 18th century, the term hackney, or *haquenée* from the Old French language, had been used for many years to describe both riding and driving horses with a comfortable trot or amble, great stamina and reliable soundness. Such was the value of these early hacks, their breeding and exportation was often restricted or even prohibited without the express permission of the monarchy.

The transformation of the old *haquenée* into the breed we recognise today took place in the early 1700s when breeders started to cross these traditional trotting types with imported Arabian stallions and Thoroughbreds. The resulting progeny gained a great deal of refinement in looks and action

Fun Facts

A smaller version, the Hackney Pony, was developed in the late 19th century by Christopher Wilson of Kirkby Lonsdale in Cumbria. Standing at about 14hh it is based on crosses between Trotters and Fell Ponies.

but lost none of the characteristics which, for so many years, had been the hallmark of the original horses.

With the gradual improvements in the quality of the nation's roads and the subsequent requirement for high quality coaching animals, efforts were concentrated on producing Hackneys for harness work. Initially the demand was purely for horses of strength, speed and stamina but it was not long until another key attribute came in to play – showmanship! With its impressive high knee action and elevated head carriage, a smart Hackney was seen as an elegant addition to a Regency gentleman's stable.

The advent of the motor car in the 20th century signalled an inevitable decline in demand for the Hackney but, to this day, it has remained a popular and desirable choice for the driving and harness enthusiasts and can frequently be seen gracing the field in showing classes across the country.

Hackney	
Place of Origin	United Kingdom
Average Height	15-15.3hh
Colour	Bay, black, brown, chestnut
Other Names	–
Uses	Driving

Haflinger

Haflinger	
Place of Origin	Austria & Italy
Average Height	13.3hh
Colour	Chestnut
Other Names	Avelignese
Uses	Dressage, vaulting, driving, general riding

The gentle Haflinger, with its distinctive chestnut colouring and flaxen mane, can trace its history back to medieval times when it was recorded that a breed of horse with Eastern origins could be found in the South Tyrolean Mountains – once Austrian but now part of present day Italy. Many theories exist as to how the oriental blood of these early mountain ponies came to reside in the remote Tyrolean valleys including the

Fun Facts

The Avelignese is the Italian equivalent of the Haflinger. Native to the country's mountainous north, it is usually a little bigger than its Austrian cousin but does share its ancestry with the stallion El' Bedavi XXII.

suggestion that their ancestors were warhorses abandoned in the 6th century by retreating Goth armies. Whatever its background there was no doubting the fact that it had adapted well to the mountain climate and terrain being strong, agile and sure-footed.

The modern Haflinger is a creation of the late 19th century. It was established in the village of Hafling in the Etschlander Mountains in 1874 with the birth of the breed's foundation stallion 249 Folie from a refined native mare and a half-Arab stallion called El' Bedavi XXII. All purebred Haflingers must be able to trace their lineage directly back to Folie through seven different stallion lines.

Haflingers have demonstrated themselves as more than willing workers capable of excelling in many fields. They will happily work in harness for driving or for pulling sleighs in their native territories. Soft of mouth and with exceptionally free paces, they can make an exceptional dressage mount for young riders, whilst their strong backs and calm, unflappable nature, makes them a frequent choice for vaulting.

Hanoverian

Hanoverian	
Place of Origin	Germany
Average Height	16.1-16.3hh
Colour	All solid colours
Other Names	-
Uses	Dressage, jumping, eventing, driving

Bred to perform at the highest level of competition in dressage, jumping, eventing and driving, the stunning Hanoverian has, over the years, earned itself a formidable reputation as equestrianism's ultimate all-rounder with few other breeds showing a similar capability to perform at the highest level of competition across such a wide breadth of disciplines.

Founded in 1735 on the stud established by George II of England at Celle in the Kingdom of Hanover, the Hanoverian was originally bred as a multi-purpose agricultural horse. With impressive stamina and substantial bone, as needs changed, by the end of the 18th century it had gained favour as an outstanding coach horse and as a worthy cavalry mount.

The invention of the motor vehicle and the disbandment of redundant

Fun Facts

The Hanoverian brand, featuring back-to-back horses in an "H" motif, has been in use at Celle since the stud was formed in 1735 by George II.

cavalry regiments saw a return to farming duties for the Hanoverian in the years that followed the First World War. Only in the years following the Second World War was the Hanoverian's sporting potential first realised and its breeding programme adapted to suit.

Today the Hanoverian's competitive credentials are without compare – in the 2008 Olympics all four riders taking gold medals in the individual and team dressage competitions were riding Hanoverians.

Highland Pony

Highland Pony	
Place of Origin	Scotland
Average Height	14hh
Colour	Grey, brown, black, bay, dun, liver chestnut
Other Names	-
Uses	General riding, showing, jumping, packhorse

The largest of Britain's nine native breeds and characterised by its distinctive dorsal stripe, the Highland Pony was first described in agricultural surveys of the 18th century; however, evidence shows that ponies have lived in the Highlands of Scotland since at least the 8th century BC and, quite possibly, for a great deal longer.

A descendent of the original crofter's ponies bred to work the beautiful yet uncompromising countryside of the Scottish Glens, the Highland Pony has been influenced by infusions of

Percheron and Spanish blood but has never been subjected to intense controlled breeding unlike many of its contemporaries.

For over 180 years Highland Ponies have been used on Scottish sporting estates to transport deer and other game off of the peaty hillsides – compact, calm and immensely strong they are easily capable of carrying up to 125kg over rough, uneven ground without difficulty. For this exact reason, they have, in more recent times, become a popular choice for pony trekking.

Very few breeds can be seen in the variety of colours experienced with the Highland Pony. In addition to the more traditional colours of grey, brown, black,

Fun Facts

Pony trekking was invented in the Scottish village of Newtonmore in 1952 by Mr Ewan Ormiston and his son Cameron. Starting from the Balavil Arms Hotel, the pair would lead small groups of riders on Highland Ponies on treks to visit the local attractions at Ruthven and Kingussie.

bay and liver chestnut they can be found in a range of duns including mouse, yellow, grey and cream.

Holsteiner

Hailing from the province of Schleswig-Holstein in the far northern reaches of Germany, the Holsteiner horse is the product of a carefully controlled systematic breeding programme that originated over 700 years ago.

The oldest of the nation's Warmblood breeds, the earliest written records of the Holsteiner date back to the 13th century at which time the monks of the city of Ütersen were granted grazing rights to land adjacent to their monastery by the Count of Holstein and Stormarn. These monks were known to breed the finest of horses – something they continued to do until Protestant Reformation of the 15th century when their land

Holsteiner	
Place of Origin	Germany
Average Height	16–17hh
Colour	All, typically bay with black points
Other Names	Holstein
Uses	Eventing, jumping, dressage

Fun Facts

In 1680 the stunning stallion Mignon was used by the Royal Stud of the Duke of Holstein to produce a strain of cream Holsteiners for the Electors of Hanover. Horses of their descent formed part of the Royal Mews at Buckingham Palace until the 1920s.

was transferred to private ownership. Fortunately for the survival of the breed, these new landowners recognised the importance and value of the Holsteiner and continued with its development.

Prized by farmers for its strength and versatility, and by the army for its courage, stamina and agility, the Holsteiner gained a significant reputation and was soon in great demand for export. However, as demand from the military dropped off, an infusion of blood from Cleveland Bay and British Yorkshire Coach Horse stallions was introduced to produce an elegant high-stepping carriage horse. Later, Thoroughbred blood was also brought into the breed bringing with it a further element of refinement and an outstanding ability to jump.

Combining smooth, balanced and elastic paces with immense scope and power, the Holsteiner has subsequently emerged as one of the world's greatest all-round sporting breeds capable of competing at the very highest level in jumping, dressage and especially eventing.

Icelandic

Located in the far North Atlantic just outside the Arctic Circle, the volcanic plateaus and fjords of Iceland were first populated in the late 9th century by Viking settlers who brought with them horses of various European origins. For centuries, other than walking, they were the only form of transport. An intrinsic part of the country's infrastructure, the horse was treated with the utmost respect.

Thanks to the remote, isolated nature of the country known as the land of ice and fire, Iceland's stock of horses remains incredibly pure – a status helped in no small part by a 930 AD declaration by Iceland's parliament, or *Althing*, that prohibits the import of any foreign horses or livestock. However, the only form of selective breeding that took place within

Fun Facts

Because of the restrictions on importing horses into Iceland it is impossible for the Icelandic Horse World Championships to be held on the island. Once a horse has been exported it can never return home.

the herds was instigated by the stallions that would fight for the best mares. Controlled breeding commenced in 1879 in what is now the country's most famous breeding area, Skagafjördur.

Icelandics are perhaps best known for their unusual gaits. In addition to the normal walk, trot, canter and gallop, they display two other paces. The most famous of these, the *tölt*, uses the same motion as the walk but at immense speed – a good Icelandic can *tölt* at up to 25mph. This pace is surprisingly comfortable to ride. When riding at *skeið*, the horse moves both legs of one side at the same time. This is considered to be a racing pace

and, when executed properly, is known as a *flugskeið*, or "flying pace".

Icelandic	
Place of Origin	Iceland
Average Height	12.3–13.2hh
Colour	Chestnut, dun, grey, black and bay
Other Names	–
Uses	General riding, ice riding

Irish Draught

Never more at home than when galloping across open country, leaping ditches and jumping over wooden rails and stone walls, the classic Irish Draught is one of the world's great sporting horses.

With ancestry that draws from the mighty French and Flemish warhorses of the 12th century Anglo–Norman invasion and Iberian and North African blood from stock imported by Spanish traders in the Middle Ages, the Irish Draught has served on farms, in harness and under saddle for the best part of 800 years. Strong and courageous, tens of thousands were exported to armies the length and breadth of the continent being used in combat right up to and including the First World War.

But it is not the Irish Draught's exploits on the battlefield that taught it its innate ability to cover ground; for that we have to thank Ireland's canny population of hunting farmers. These hardy men wanted a mount that could work on the land and pull the cart to church for Sunday mass but also, and in their minds most importantly, carry them for a full day's fox hunting and take with ease any brook, fence or fallen tree that might hinder their progress. An old Irish rhyme describes how it should "plough, sow, reap and mow, go to church and hunt!"

All this inherent experience has led to the Irish Draught of today being a sensible animal with

Irish Draught	
Place of Origin	Ireland
Average Height	16–17hh
Colour	All solid colours
Other Names	-
Uses	Jumping, hunting, general riding

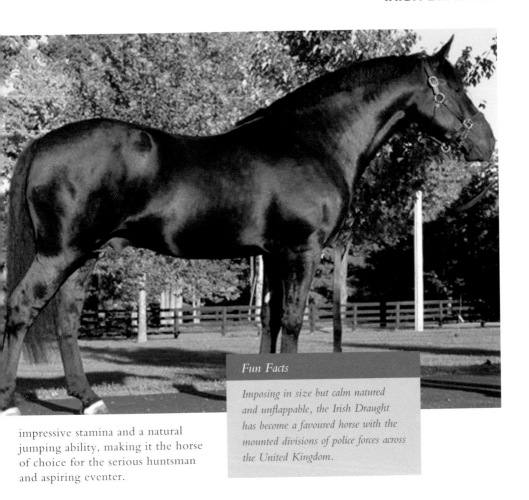

Fun Facts

Imposing in size but calm natured and unflappable, the Irish Draught has become a favoured horse with the mounted divisions of police forces across the United Kingdom.

impressive stamina and a natural jumping ability, making it the horse of choice for the serious huntsman and aspiring eventer.

Irish Sport Horse

Ever since the "invention" of show jumping in Ireland in the second half of the 19th century, the versatile Irish Draught has made its mark the world over. Breeders, however, were not slow to recognise that for competitive purposes, the breed could still be improved. With an infusion of Thoroughbred blood adding its inherent speed and endurance to the Draught's unflappable temperament and matchless jumping ability they were able to produce what is arguably the ultimate sporting all-rounder.

First known as the Irish Hunter and now universally as the Irish Sport Horse (ISH), the breed dominates the upper echelons of international competition winning regularly at the highest levels of show jumping and eventing and is even beginning to show its colours in the dressage arena. In 2008, eight of the horses to medal in the individual and team eventing were Irish Sport Horses – four of those belonging to British team riders. Such is their prowess, the Irish Sport Horse Studbook has been ranked first in the WBSFH eventing rankings for 13 consecutive years.

The Irish Sport Horse has a

Irish Sport Horse	
Place of Origin	Ireland
Average Height	16-17hh
Colour	Any
Other Names	Irish Hunter, Irish Horse
Uses	Eventing, jumping, hunting

Fun Facts

The Irish Sport Horse is classified into three types: lightweight for carrying a rider up to about 70kg, middleweight to carry a rider up to about 89kg, and heavyweight for riders exceeding 89kg.

wonderful calm temperament. Honest
but lively and energetic when required,
it displays excellent stamina whilst
retaining all of the fiery jumping ability
of its Draught relations.

Knabstrupper

The eye-catching spotted Knabstrupper was first established at the time of the Napoleonic Wars after a butcher by the name of Flaebe purchased a mare from a Spanish cavalry officer that he simply named Flaebehoppen – Flaebe's Horse. Flaebehoppen was unusually coloured for her time, being a dark red chestnut with a white mane and tail and small white snowflakes covering her entire body.

Flaebe sold the mare to a local judge, titular councillor of state Major Villars Lunn, who was the owner of the Knabstrup Hovedgaard, a grandiose manor house situated in Holbaek, Nordsealand, where she was put to work in the fields and in harness. Having been noted for her strength, speed and stamina, the mare was then bred to a chestnut Frederiksborg stallion producing a spectacular metallic coloured colt, Flaebehingsten, who would become the foundation stallion for the breed. So dramatic were his markings, his colour was often described as being green!

The Knabstrupper became known

Knabstrupper	
Place of Origin	Denmark
Average Height	15.2-15.3hh
Colour	White with brown or black spots
Other Names	Knabstrup
Uses	Dressage, jumping, eventing, general riding

Fun Facts

Sometimes the Knabstrupper could prove a little too eye catching. A favourite of Danish cavalry officers during the 1848-1850 Schleswig War, it had the effect of singling them out for snipers – a little like hanging a target on your back!

for its impressive paces, calm nature and general hardiness – all fine attributes in a horse – but it was its head-turning appearance that made it highly desirable.

There are four recognised varieties of modern Knabstrupper. Whilst the Classic, Pony and Miniature are regarded as general riding types, the Sport Horse has been developed by crossing with other European Warmbloods to compete at the very highest level in jumping, eventing and especially dressage.

Lipizzaner

Instantly recognisable and forever associated with the world famous Spanish Riding School of Vienna, the elegant Lipizzaner was first bred in 1580. At the behest of Archduke Charles II of Austria, a private imperial stud was established at Lipizza (now called Lipica in what is part of the Karst region of modern day Slovenia) to service the nine stallions and 24 mares. His desire was to produce grand horses for the Imperial stables at Graz and Vienna.

Born either black or dark brown,

Lipizzaners gradually lighten in colour until, aged between 6 and 10 years old, they finally turn grey. Although rare, very occasionally a bay Lipizzaner may be born, one of which is always kept in the stables in Vienna.

Although now bred at a number of stud farms across Austria, Hungary and Slovenia, it is the horses of the Piber Stud near Graz that are now used by the Spanish Riding School. Each stallion is selected having already proven itself over many years at the School whilst each mare must first undergo extensive performance testing.

The Spanish Riding School of Vienna is the oldest surviving establishment of its kind in the

Lipizzaner	
Place of Origin	Austria & Slovenia
Average Height	15.1–16.2hh
Colour	Grey
Other Names	Lipizzan
Uses	Dressage, driving

world. Founded in 1572, its purpose has essentially remained the same throughout its long and illustrious existence – that being to keep alive the noble art of classical horsemanship from generation to generation. Tradition aside, to this day the school has found no horse more suitable for performing the "airs above the ground" than the Lipizzaner.

Lusitano

Originating from the often mountainous terrain of the Iberian Peninsula, known to the Romans as Lusitania, the Lusitano is one of the most agile of all horse breeds in existence today. Lightning fast, courageous and possessing an innate ability to maintain balance at all times and to twist and turn in seemingly impossible circles, it has, for many generations, been the favoured mount of both the Portuguese cavalry and the *rejoneadore* – Portugal's own horseback bullfighters.

Sharing similar ancestry to its Andalusian neighbour (see page 32), the Lusitano is a cooperative and highly trainable breed with impressive elevated paces and a naturally crested head carriage – all attributes that have contributed to it becoming highly suited to the technical aerial movements of *Haute École* and, in turn, seen its desirability as a dressage horse increase dramatically in recent years.

Perhaps the most famous Lusitano was the grey stallion Novilheiro. Foaled in Portugal in 1971, he progressed to Grand Prix level dressage in the United States. He then travelled to England where he competed as an intermediate level event horse before catching the eye of international show jumper and Olympic rider John Whitaker. Within a year of changing discipline, the talented 10-year-old was competing at open Grand Prix level before taking the British title in 1983.

Lusitano	
Place of Origin	Portugal
Average Height	15-16hh
Colour	Any solid colour but usually grey
Other Names	-
Uses	Dressage, bullfighting, driving

Fun Facts

Lusitanos are said to possess incredibly smooth paces – so much so that it is even possible to hold a full glass of wine whilst in piaffe without spilling a drop!

Morgan

The spirited Morgan horse is known to have originated in the town of West Springfield, Massachusetts, in 1789, with a bay colt called Figure. As a yearling, the young horse was given as settlement of a debt to Justin Morgan, a schoolmaster from Vermont. When mature, Morgan, as the horse was renamed, began to show surprising versatility, becoming widely known and acknowledged for his stump pulling ability, strength and stamina when ploughing and ease of use under saddle or in harness.

Fortunately for future generations, Morgan showed an unusual level of prepotency – the genetic ability to pass one's physical appearance and innate qualities to offspring. Of Morgan's progeny, the stallions Bullrush, Sherman and Woodbury became the most influential with all present day Morgan Horses being traceable to these three.

Fun Facts

The Morgan horse is the official state animal of Vermont and the state horse of Massachusetts.

By the 1820s, the Morgan was dominating the burgeoning horse industry of the states of New York and New England as the favoured choice for agricultural work, stage coach teams and for general transportation. During the American Civil War, it saw action for both the North and South as a cavalry horse and as a mount for the Union General Philip H Sheridan and the Confederacy's Stonewall Jackson.

The modern day Morgan excels as a show horse in its native country and has made an impact on the international scene as a formidable competitor in the dressage arena and over jumps.

Morgan	
Place of Origin	United States
Average Height	14.1–15.2hh
Colour	Bay, black, brown, chestnut
Other Names	-
Uses	Dressage, jumping, driving, hunting

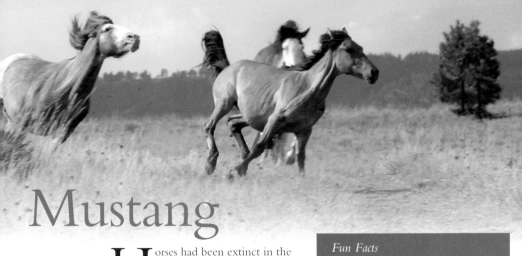

Mustang

Horses had been extinct in the Americas for over 10,000 years when the Spanish Conquistadors landed in the 15th and 16th centuries bringing with them mighty Barbs, Sorraia and Andalusians. As the Pueblo Indians revolted in 1680 to force a Spanish retreat, many thousands of these were set free and never recaptured. These *mesteño* or *mestengo*, meaning stray or ownerless, horses were to form the basis of what we now know as the Mustang – the iconic free-spirited breed of the American West.

Over the centuries, these herds grew to a phenomenal size occasionally receiving infusions of fresh blood from the miscellany of draught horses and cowboy ponies that had escaped from the countless settlers who were arriving by the day from the East. By the turn of the 20th century, it is estimated that the Mustang population had reached close to two million. However, a population of this size required a considerable amount of food and grazing, demand from the East was pushing up the price of beef and something had to give. Before long the ranchers, who for so long had been associated with the fortitude of the Mustang, started to shoot them in large numbers until, by 1970, there were fewer than 17,000 remaining.

Declaring that the Mustang was a "living symbol of the historic and pioneer spirit of the West", the United States Congress finally took long overdue action in 1971 by passing an act to protect the future of the breed.

Mustang	
Place of Origin	United States
Average Height	13.2-15hh
Colour	All colours
Other Names	-
Uses	Wild (feral)

New Forest Pony

New Forest Pony	
Place of Origin	Hampshire, England
Average Height	14.2hh
Colour	Any colour
Other Names	Forester
Uses	General riding, jumping

Fun Facts

Lord Lucas, the "improver" of the New Forest Pony, was quite a sportsman. On Boxing Day, 1913, he rode his own Forester, a mare called The Nun, to a six-length victory in a "take your own line" point-to-point at Picket Post. Not bad going for a man who had lost a leg fighting in the Boer War!

Although King Canute's Forest Law of 1016 makes mention of the presence of horses grazing wild in Forests of Wessex, the precise origins of the New Forest Pony are lost in the mists of time. This, however, has made little difference to a pony that, largely due to geography, has been subjected to the influence of countless other equine breeds at some point in its history. Not that this has been to the New Forest Pony's detriment with the breed remaining as hardy and as popular as ever.

The first effort to intentionally develop the horse stock of the New Forest was in 1208 when 18 Welsh mares were introduced. Further improvements were attempted in the 18th century with Thoroughbred blood being added, whilst in the 19th century, Queen Victoria loaned two Arab stallions, Zorah and Abeyan, and the Barb, Yuresson.

The biggest improvements to the breed came thanks to the innovative efforts of Lord Arthur Cecil and Lord

Lucas. Concerned that the New Forest Pony was beginning to lack durability and substance, they introduced Galloways, Highlands, Fells, Dales and Dartmoors into the equation with the addition in 1918 of blood from the polo pony stallion Field Marshall. Incredibly, from this curious concoction the New Forest Pony as we recognise it today started to emerge.

Although all privately owned, numerous "Foresters" still spend their days roaming wild within the New Forest – a National Park since 2005. Others, usually stud or privately bred, are in extensive use as general riding ponies being suitable for both children and adults to handle with ease.

Norwegian Fjord

Norwegian Fjord	
Place of Origin	Norway
Average Height	13-14hh
Colour	Dun with black dorsal stripe
Other Names	Vestlandshest, Nordfjordhest
Uses	General riding, driving, agriculture

Resplendent with a black dorsal stripe from forelock to tail and bearing a striking resemblance to the wild Asiatic Przewalski, the Norwegian Fjord is one of the most distinctive of all domestic horse breeds. Retaining its original primitive character and colouring, it remains one of the purest and oldest breeds in the world. The mount of Viking warriors, it was no stranger to travelling by sea and has undoubtedly had a historical influence on the indigenous breeds of the United Kingdom and the Icelandic Pony.

In its native Norway, the Fjord has long been known as a highly robust pony with a strong back and an amenable nature willing to take on any task asked of it. Sure-footed, expert at traversing the precarious mountain tracks of its homeland and seemingly oblivious to harsh weather, it can still be found year-round working in harness with cart or plough or pack, demonstrating an ability to go where no tractor or 4x4 dare tread.

It would be wrong, however, to say

Fun Facts

When Norway hosted the Winter Olympics at Lillehammer in 1994, the Fjord had an important part to play. Along with two other native breeds, the Døl and the Nordland, it was used to transport competitors from the Olympic village over the snow-packed roads to their events.

that the modern Fjord's abilities begin and end with the harness. With limitless stamina and a smooth, light action it excels at endurance and has also proven itself a capable contender in the dressage arena.

Oldenburg

T he deep chested, powerfully built Oldenburg, the heaviest of the German Warmblood breeds, was first established in the 17th century by Count Anton Günther von Oldenburg. Working from a base of Friesian mares he imported blood from Spanish, Barbs and Neapolitans collected on his extensive European travels, with the intention of producing a grand and imposing carriage horse. During the 19th century further crosses were made to introduce characteristics of the Thoroughbred, Cleveland Bay and Hanoverian. The product was a heavyweight but, nevertheless, agile and athletic coach horse that stood a good 17hh. With the invention of the motor car, the strong and willing Oldenburgs had no difficulty adapting to a new role as a general purpose farm horse.

During the 1960s the Oldenburg's breeding association, the Verband der Züchter des Oldenburger Pferdes, made the decision to update the Oldenburg with a view to producing a more general riding horse with outstanding sporting potential. The top European Thoroughbred stallions were chosen to improve the breed's speed and general refinement whilst others, including Anglo-Arabs, Trakehners and Holsteiners, were utilised to enhance paces and jumping ability.

The resulting sport horse is now one of the world's most successful and can be seen competing and winning medals at Olympic level in dressage, eventing and show jumping.

Oldenburg	
Place of Origin	Germany
Average Height	16.2–17.2hh
Colour	Bay, black, brown
Other Names	Alt-Oldenburger
Uses	Dressage, jumping, eventing, driving

Palomino

Described as having the appearance of a newly minted gold coin, the Palomino is unique in the equestrian world in that, rather than being a true breed, it is actually a colour type. However, thanks largely to the efforts of the Palomino Horse Association, it has achieved near breed status, being shown, bred and registered in its own right.

Although widely attributed to the United States, palomino coloured horses have existed across the globe throughout equine history featuring (by description) in the Old Testament book of Zechariah and having appeared in art from 2nd century BC China through to the works of Botticelli. It was the invading Spanish Conquistadors who first introduced the palomino colour to the Americas.

The Palomino Horse Association was created in California in 1935, with the registration of Dick Haliday's magnificent golden stallion *El Rey de los Reyes* – the King of Kings. It does not discriminate against any breed, with registration being based upon conformation and colouring – a golden coat with a mane and tail either of white, ivory or silver.

A true multi-purpose horse, the Palomino can be found participating in anything and everything from ranching and rodeo through to trail rides, jumping and even racing.

Palomino	
Place of Origin	United States
Average Height	14.1–16hh
Colour	Palomino
Other Names	-
Uses	Showing, ranching, western riding

Fun Facts

"Happy trails!" In its time the Palomino has had quite a career as a film star! Roy Rogers' courageous horse Trigger was a Palomino as was Mr Ed the talking horse.

Paso Fino / Peruvian Paso

Although the modern Paso Fino and Peruvian Paso share a common ancestry to the Barb, Spanish Jennet and Andalusian, they were actually introduced to the New World by completely different groups of 17th century Spanish settlers, in contrasting environments and for quite different tasks.

The Paso Fino's heritage lies around Central and South America and the

the mountainous Peruvian interior.

Famous for their *brio,* an innate desire and ability to work tirelessly for their rider, both breeds display the same conformation and elegant high head carriage but their defining feature is their *termino* – a distinctive high and free-flowing four-beat lateral gait in which the horse's forelegs swing out to the side rather than moving in straight strides. Of these, the *Paso Corto* is the normal gait for travel, the *Paso Largo* is an extended gait for speed and the magnificent *Paso Fino* is a slow, elevated and highly collected gait for no other reason than to impress onlookers.

Caribbean where it was initially bred as a mount for the Conquistadors before being adopted by the region's wealthy and ambitious plantation owners who hailed it for its remarkable endurance and comfortable gaits.

Similar in appearance, the Peruvian Paso is also a product of the Spanish colonisation of the Americas. Selective breeding created a horse that was both light and agile, whilst possessing remarkable sure-footedness and stamina – the ideal mount for long days in the saddle negotiating the steep and rocky passes of

Paso Fino / Peruvian Paso	
Place of Origin	Central & South America
Average Height	14–15hh
Colour	Bay, chestnut
Other Names	-
Uses	General riding, endurance, ranching

Percheron

An undisputed heavyweight champion of the horse world, the magnificently handsome Percheron has long owned a reputation as the ultimate equestrian powerhouse. Although the breed's precise origins remain unknown, it is often thought that its ancestors were Arabian and Barb warhorses abandoned by the defeated Umayyad Caliphate Moors after the Battle of Poitiers in 732 AD, which were subsequently crossed with massive Flemish horses owned by breeders in the French province of Perche. A further infusion of Arab blood was introduced after the First Crusade in 1099.

Initially used as a heavy warhorse, the advent of gunpowder saw its primary use change to that of a heavy draught both on the farm and on the battlefield where it could pull with ease the

Percheron	
Place of Origin	France
Average Height	16.2-17hh
Colour	Dapple-grey or Black
Other Names	-
Uses	Heavy draught

Fun Facts

Foaled in 1902, the Percheron, Dr Le Gear, was the largest horse ever recorded. Standing at 21hh, he weighed in at an astonishing 1,372kg – about the same as a Vauxhall Corsa!

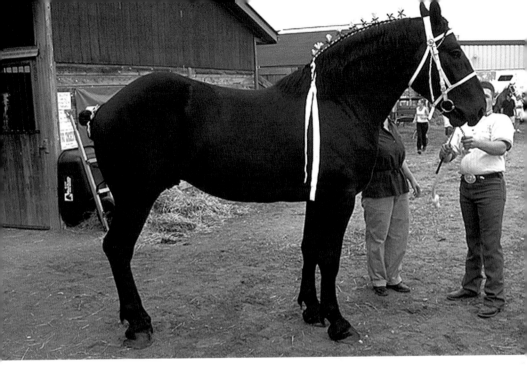

immense, heavy artillery pieces of the day. When France needed a horse to pull its heavy passenger and mail coaches, the Percheron, able to trot at a steady pace for endless miles, fitted the bill perfectly. With the French coaches known as *diligences*, the breed, for a time, became known as the Diligence Horse.

The advent of the railways saw the Percheron revert to its role as farm tractor and artillery horse where it remained immensely popular. Thousands were exported to the United States to a point where, in the 1930s, over 70 per cent of the purebred draught horses working in North America, were Percheron.

Although some modern day Percherons can be found working in the fields, their numbers are few; most being used instead, for showing.

Przewalski's
Horse (Takhi)

A highly endangered species, the Przewalski's Horse (also known as the Takhi) was first discovered living in the wild in 1878, by the Russian geographer, Colonel Nikolai Mikhailovich Przhevalsky, on an exploratory trip to Mongolia's Takhin Shaar Nuruu mountains, bordering the Gobi Desert.

At the time it was the world's last remaining truly wild and undomesticated breed of horse – other breeds such as the American Mustang and Australian Brumby, whilst often considered to be "wild", are actually feral having been descended from once domesticated stock. Although for many years there were

Przewalski's Horse (Takhi)	
Place of Origin	Asia
Average Height	12-14hh
Colour	Beige-brown or dun
Other Names	Takhi, Mongolian or Asian Wild Horse
Uses	Undomesticated

Fun Facts

Many believe the Przewalski to be the direct ancestor of the modern domestic horse but others claim this is not possible and that it is a completely different species, having 66 chromosomes as opposed to 64. The Przewalski, however, can be successfully crossed with domestic breeds – the resulting fertile offspring carrying a unique 65 chromosomes.

many reported sightings of wild Takhi herds, following the Second World War their numbers took a turn for the worse. The result is that not one Takhi herd has been seen since 1967.

Fortunately for the survival of the breed, a good number of Takhis were taken into captivity at the turn of the 20th century, including 12 which were taken to the Woburn Estate of the Duke of Bedford. With such a limited base of horses to work with, breeding in captivity has been a difficult process; furthermore, inbreeding can be a potential harbinger of congenital defects and disease. In an endeavour to save the breed from further decline, attempts are now being made to return the Takhi to the wild.

The heavily built Takhi is highly distinctive and bears a black dorsal "eel" stripe along the length of its back, striped legs and an erect brush-like mane which, unlike that of the Norwegian Fjord, does not fall flat if left uncut.

Selle Français

The epitome of the modern classic sport horse, the Selle Français is regarded as one of the most athletic and tractable breeds in existence today. Like so many European performance breeds it is a Warmblood and a combination of many years of selected crossbreeding; however, what sets it aside from the competition is the strong influence of the trotting breeds that make up its formidable historic bloodline.

In the late 19th century, breeders around the government-managed Normandy stud farms at Le Pin and Saint Lô, actively imported quality English Thoroughbred Norfolk Trotter stallions with which to improve their hardy Norman stock. The result was the speedy French Trotter harness horse and the Anglo-Norman in both draught and saddle types; the latter of which was to become the basis of the Selle Français.

In the years following the Second World War, with demand for general riding and draught horses in decline, the French began to concentrate on the production of a performance horse that could display speed, stamina and sporting ability. To strengthen ongoing bloodlines it was decided in 1958 to merge the Breton, Vendéen, Charolais and Demi-Sang du Centre with the Anglo-Norman under a single name, *le cheval de Selle Français* – the French

Saddle Horse.

The Selle Français has gone on to become one of the most talented and desirable of all competition horses and has excelled at the highest levels in show jumping, eventing and dressage. Some horses have also been bred specifically to race as AQPSA (Autres Que Pur Sang Association, meaning "other than Thoroughbred").

Because of its diverse origin, the conformation of the Selle Français can vary dramatically from horse to horse but is usually found to be deep-chested, strong and muscular with an attractive head set on a long neck.

Selle Français	
Place of Origin	France
Average Height	Variable depending on type
Colour	Usually chestnut
Other Names	French Saddle Horse, French Warmblood
Uses	Jumping, eventing, dressage, racing

Shetland Pony

The smallest of all the British pony breeds, the Shetland has lived a tough existence on the unforgiving, craggy and gale battered Shetland Isles for many thousands of years. It is thought to have origins in the ancient Cob type of Tundra and the Mountain Ponies of southern Europe that migrated to Scandinavia and the north across the vast ice fields of the last glacial age. The later introduction of ponies brought to the islands by visiting Celts and Vikings, is said to have defined the breed. Local excavations have revealed the Bronze Age remains of ponies that are thought to have been in domestic use.

Shetland Pony	
Place of Origin	Scotland
Average Height	40in (Shetlands are measured in inches not hands)
Colour	Black, brown, chestnut, grey
Other Names	-
Uses	General riding, driving

Fun Facts

Since 1956 the British Army's Parachute Regiment has had a Shetland as its mascot. The role is currently held by a black gelding named Pegasus.

The remote nature of the Shetland Isles, located in the North Sea 100 miles northeast of Scotland and just 400 miles south of the Arctic Circle, has meant that, over the years, there has been little importation of other breeds and, as such, the native Shetland Pony remains every inch the hardy animal it has always been. Two distinct types have developed – one heavier boned with a long head, the other smaller, lighter and rather more pretty to the eye. Both have for centuries provided efficient transport and strong labour to the Shetland Islanders.

The modern Shetland can usually be found in employment as either a children's riding pony or in harness for carriage driving – steady temperament being ideal for both. Despite their naturally calm nature, they are supremely courageous and will happily take on jumps that appear to far exceed the capabilities of their diminutive but rotund proportions.

Shire

The tallest of all the heavy draught breeds, the mighty Shire Horse has, for centuries, worked in close harmony with his human counterparts on the fields and roads of Britain. His ancestor was the medieval Great Horse, the heavyweight war machine that, in 1066, had accompanied William the

Conqueror and his invading forces.

Finding extensive use as a draught horse, a distinctive variation of the Great Horse, bolstered by imported types from the Netherlands, emerged across the eastern counties of England during the 17th century. Known as the English Black it showed immense strength but was dull in colour and rather sluggish. The most significant changes occurred thanks to the input of the renowned breeder, Robert Bakewell, who, in the late 18th century, imported six Flanders mares to improve the line to create the "Bakewell Black". With the founding of the pedigree society in 1878, the breed became known as the English Cart Horse but this was changed to the Shire six years later.

For many years the Shire was a common sight in the English countryside and on the busy city streets. There were few sights more popular than that of a team of Shires pulling a brewer's dray full of ale from pub to pub – a tradition maintained to this day by several breweries across the United Kingdom. But, as with so many breeds, the onset of mechanisation in the 20th century saw numbers fall into sharp decline. Fortunately, however, the breed has remained immensely popular and numbers are now, once again, on the rise.

Fun Facts

Two Shires were put to the test at the 1924 Wembley Exhibition when they were fastened to a dynameter – a special piece of equipment designed to measure pulling power. Unfortunately we will never know the result of their exploits as the machine became overloaded and broke when they exceeded 50 tonnes!

Shire

Place of Origin	United Kingdom
Average Height	17.2hh
Colour	Black, bay, brown, grey
Other Names	-
Uses	Heavy draught

Suffolk Punch

The oldest of Britain's heavy horse breeds, the Suffolk Punch has remained wonderfully pure throughout its history thanks to the isolated nature of its place of origin, the East Anglian counties of Norfolk and Suffolk; a highly agricultural area, surrounded on three sides by the North Sea.

Dating from the 16th century, all Suffolks alive today can trace their male lineage back to a single stallion, Thomas Crisp's Horse of Ufford, who was foaled

in 1768. The earlier ancestry of this horse is unknown but it is thought that imported heavy horses from the Low Countries and the ubiquitous Norfolk Trotter must have played their part.

The Suffolk Punch was developed for one reason and one reason only – to work as the ultimate piece of farm machinery amongst the heavy, thick clay soils of the East Anglian countryside. Short coupled, heavy boned and with clean, featherless legs it was ideally suited to the task. The Suffolk's trademark is its astonishing pulling technique – the horse can willingly drop right down onto its knees to lower its centre of gravity and maximise power output.

Suffolk Punch	
Place of Origin	East Anglia, United Kingdom
Average Height	16-16.3hh
Colour	Chesnut
Other Names	Suffolk Horse
Uses	Heavy draught

Numbers have declined dramatically since the onset of mechanisation in the second half of the 20th century but, with renewed interest being shown in all the heavy horse breeds, they are steadily on the rise once more.

Thoroughbred

Thoroughbred	
Place of Origin	United Kingdom
Average Height	16-16.3hh
Colour	Bay, black, brown, chestnut, grey
Other Names	-
Uses	Racing, jumping, dressage

In the years since it was first developed, the Thoroughbred has had but a single task – to run as fast as possible. The fact that it fulfils this requirement in somewhat spectacular fashion, has led, in no small way, to it achieving the status as the world's most valuable breed of horse.

All Thoroughbreds can trace their pedigree back to three stallions – the Byerley Turk, the Darley Arabian and the Godolphin Arabian – each of which was named after their respective owners – Captain Robert Byerley, Thomas Darley and the Lord Godolphin. All three were brought to England in the 17th and 18th centuries and put to mares from stronger native breeds such as the Irish Hobby. The result was a creature that could sustain a great pace for a considerable time but that still had substantial weight-carrying abilities.

Since those early days, the Thoroughbred has gone on to become one of the world's most well known and successful breeds – there is barely a race in existence that has not, at some point, been won by a relative, however distant,

Fun Facts

In February 2006 at the Fasig-Tipton Calder sale in Florida, a two-year-old Thoroughbred Colt called the Green Monkey was sold to Irish billionaire John Magnier for an astonishing $16million – an all time record price for a horse sold at auction.

of the Byerley, Darley or Godolphin.

The Thoroughbred has also had a significant influence on countless other breeds, from the Irish Sport Horse and American Quarter Horse to the Selle Français – its impact has been universal.

In addition to racing, the Thoroughbred has proved itself in many other competitive and non-competitive disciplines. Many compete in eventing, jumping and dressage right up to Olympic level, whilst others are employed across the world as police horses, and few would pass on the chance to partake in a day's hunting.

Trakehner

The noble Trakehner, renowned for its athleticism, intelligence and friendly demeanour, is one of the oldest German Warmblood breeds having been established at the Trakehnen Stud of King Friedrich Wilhelm I of Prussia in 1732. Originally a fast, sound cavalry mount, it was developed by crossing small local native mares called Schwaike, with English Thoroughbreds and purebred Arabians. With more average examples being sold off locally as general riding horses, incredibly strict selection permitted only the very best to breed. The result has a distinctive and supremely high quality horse with elite credentials.

In the years following the First World War, the breed's potential as a competition horse began to come to light and, in the 1920s and 30s, Trakehners won gold and silver medals at two Olympic Games and took victory in the *Velka Pardubicka* Steeplechase, possibly the world's most daunting and notorious horse race, on nine occasions.

In October 1944, with Stalin's Soviet forces fast advancing through Germany, permission was given to evacuate the

Trakehner	
Place of Origin	Germany
Average Height	16-16.2hh
Colour	Any solid colour
Other Names	East Prussian
Uses	Dressage, jumping, eventing

stud. Their 1,450km march to the west sent the horses on an arduous journey across the frozen Vistula Lagoon. Although many did not survive *der Treck*, the western exodus meant that the breed was saved, unlike the Trakehnen Stud which, following the war, was abandoned and left to decay.

The modern Trakehner continues to be a top class performance horse. With an elegant, floating trot and wonderfully soft and balanced canter, it excels at dressage, whilst powerful hindquarters and strong joints, make it a supreme jumper both in the arena and cross-country. All in all, a better sport horse would be hard to find.

Welsh Pony and Cob

The Welsh Pony and Cob Society was established in 1901 by farmers and landowners who recognised the importance of documenting the country's own mountain and cob breeds. Horses and ponies entered in its studbook are classified in one of four sections:

Section A for Welsh Mountain Ponies under 12hh, Section B for Welsh Ponies under 13.2hh, Section C for Welsh Ponies (Cob type) under 13.2hh and Section D for Welsh Cobs over 13.2hh.

The Welsh Mountain Pony may give the impression of being light and delicate but having been bred in the

Welsh Pony and Cob	
Place of Origin	Wales
Average Height	Dependent on type – see text
Colour	Grey, bay, chestnut
Other Names	-
Uses	Riding, driving

Fun Facts

During the reign of Henry VIII, several laws were passed that forbade the use of horses under 15hh for breeding. Fortunately for the survival of the Welsh Pony, the rugged, inhospitable and often remote nature of its homeland meant that horses were relatively easy to keep hidden so it was largely left undisturbed.

remote and wild Welsh mountains for generations, it is, in truth, a hardy, sound and constitutionally strong little creature. A big horse in a little body! Eager to please and perform, it is a superb child's ride but is never better than when working in a scurry harness where it can display its amazing strength, speed and ability.

The Welsh Cob and Cob type, aptly known as "the best ride and drive animal in the world", has been bred over the centuries for its strength, resilience and stamina. It retains the pony character of its smaller cousins whilst proving itself more than competent in the sporting arena. All Welsh types love to jump!

The pictures in this book were provided courtesy of the following:

GETTY IMAGES
www.gettyimages.co.uk

SHUTTERSTOCK
www.shutterstock.com

Design and artwork by David Wildish and Scott Giarnese

Published by G2 Entertainment Limited

Publishers Jules Gammond and Edward Adams

Written by Jon Stroud